The Puzz

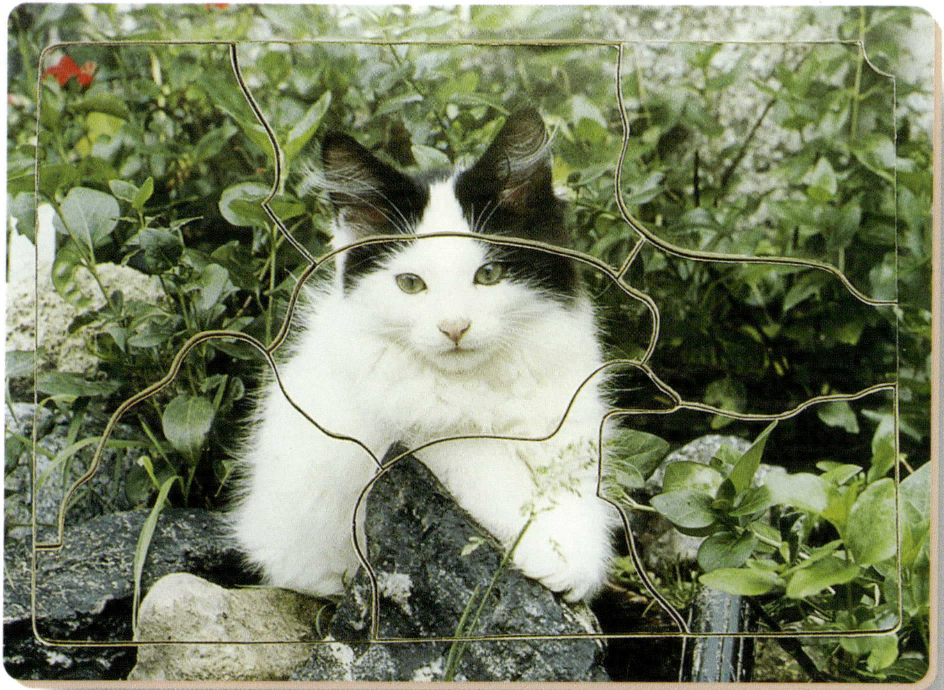

Where does this go?

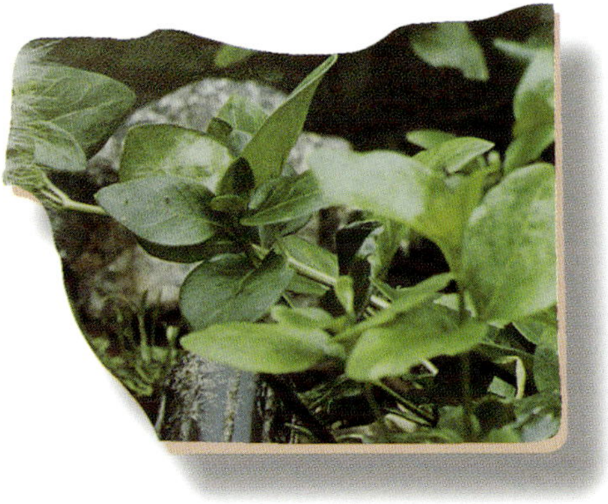

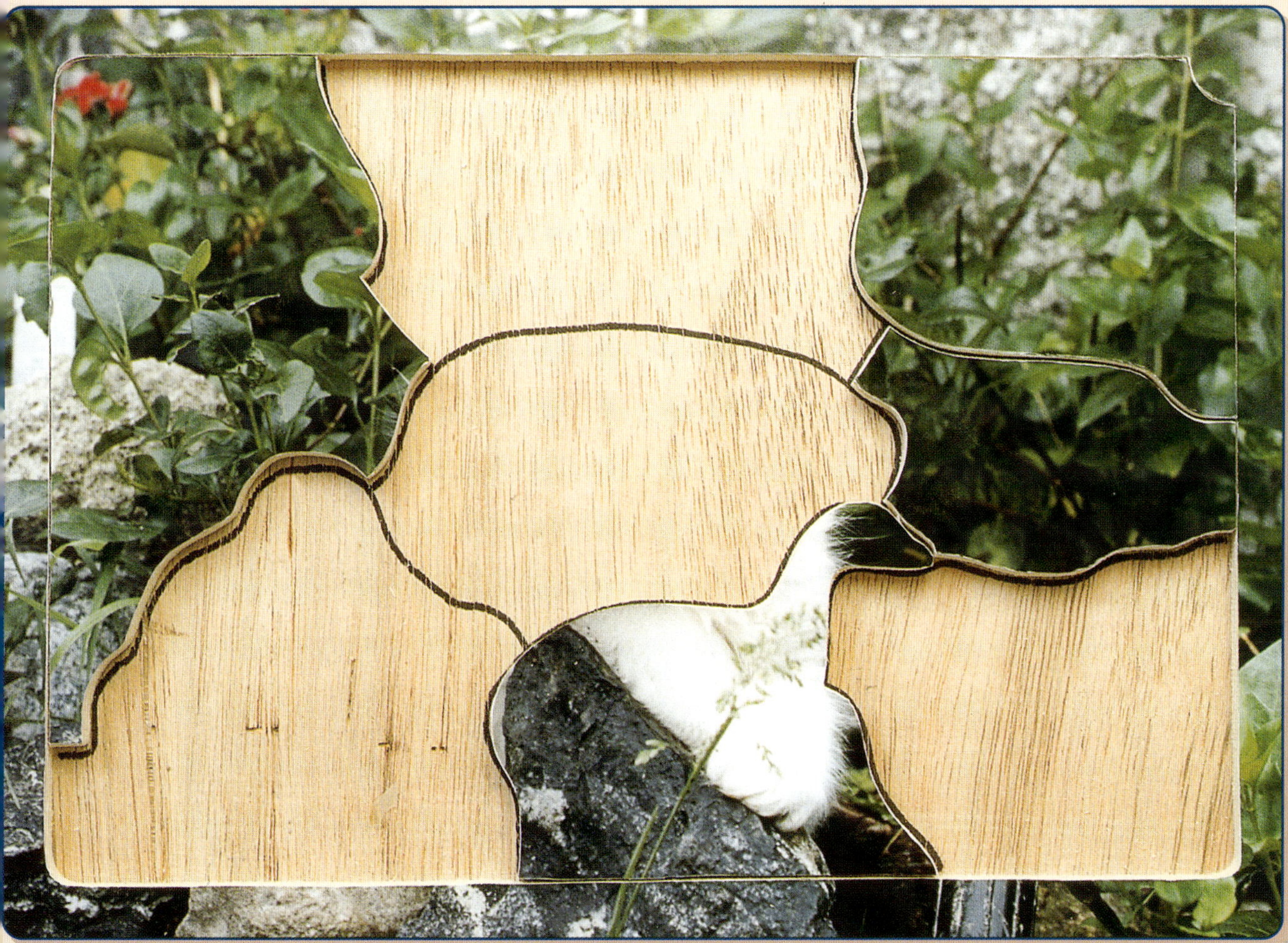

It goes here.

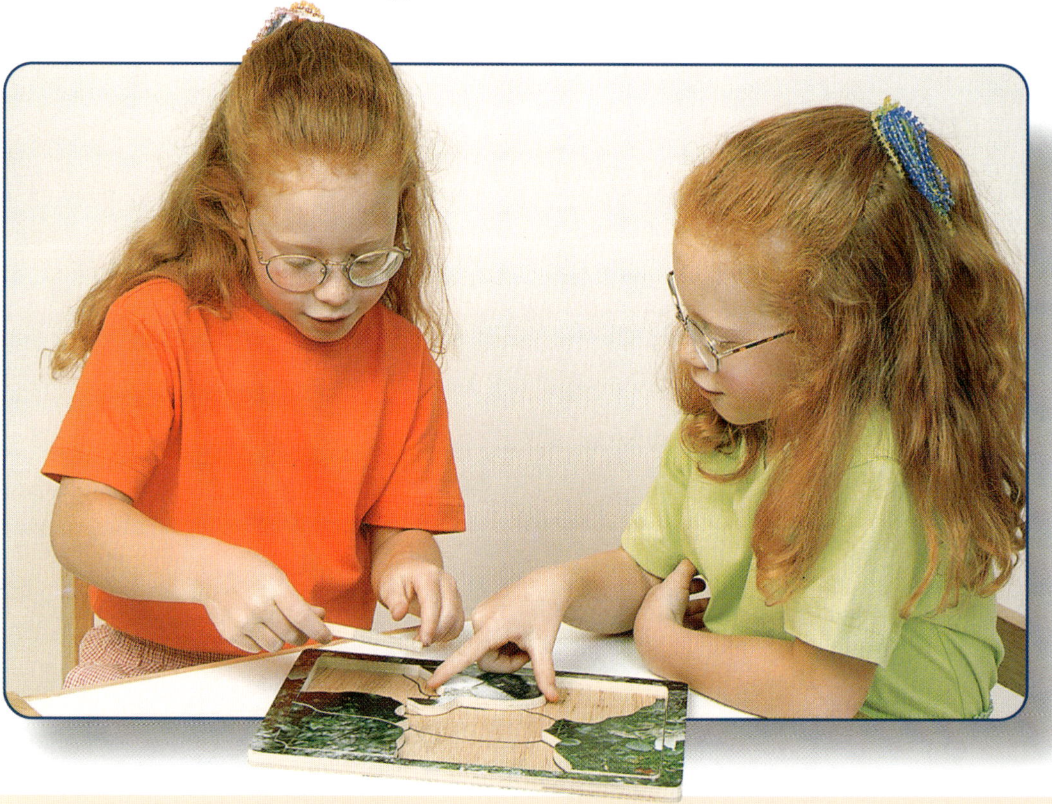

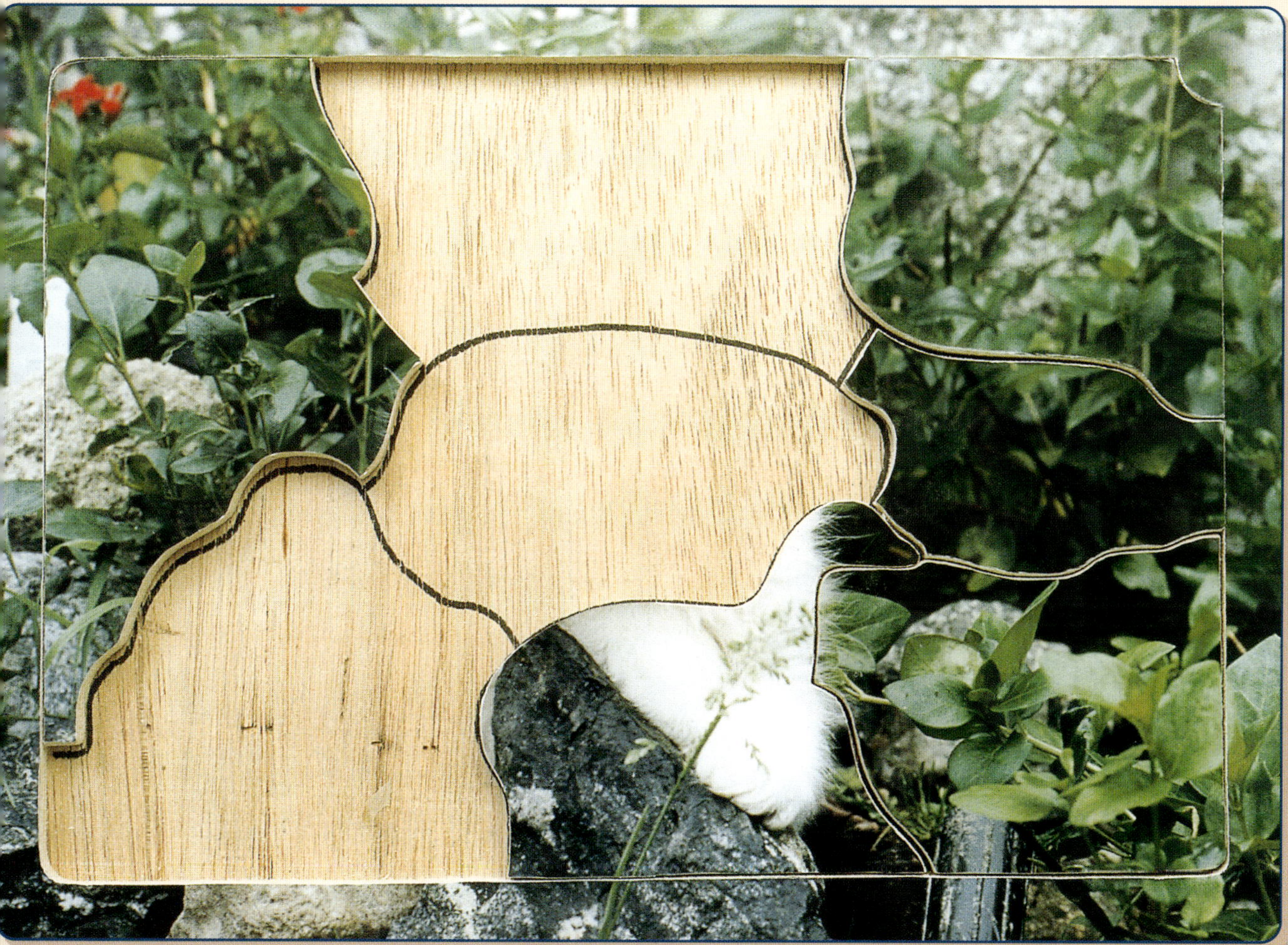

Where does this go?

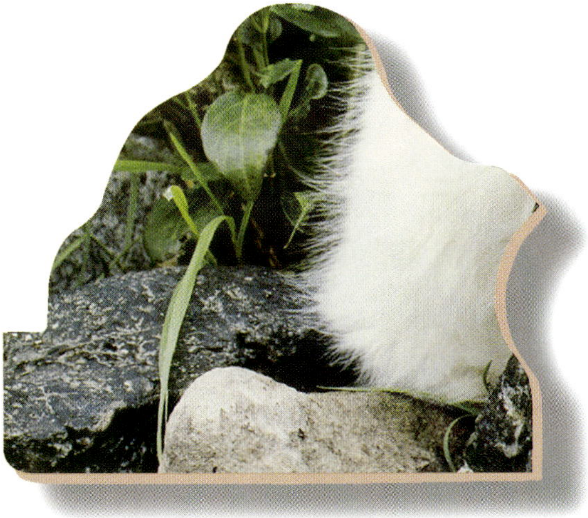

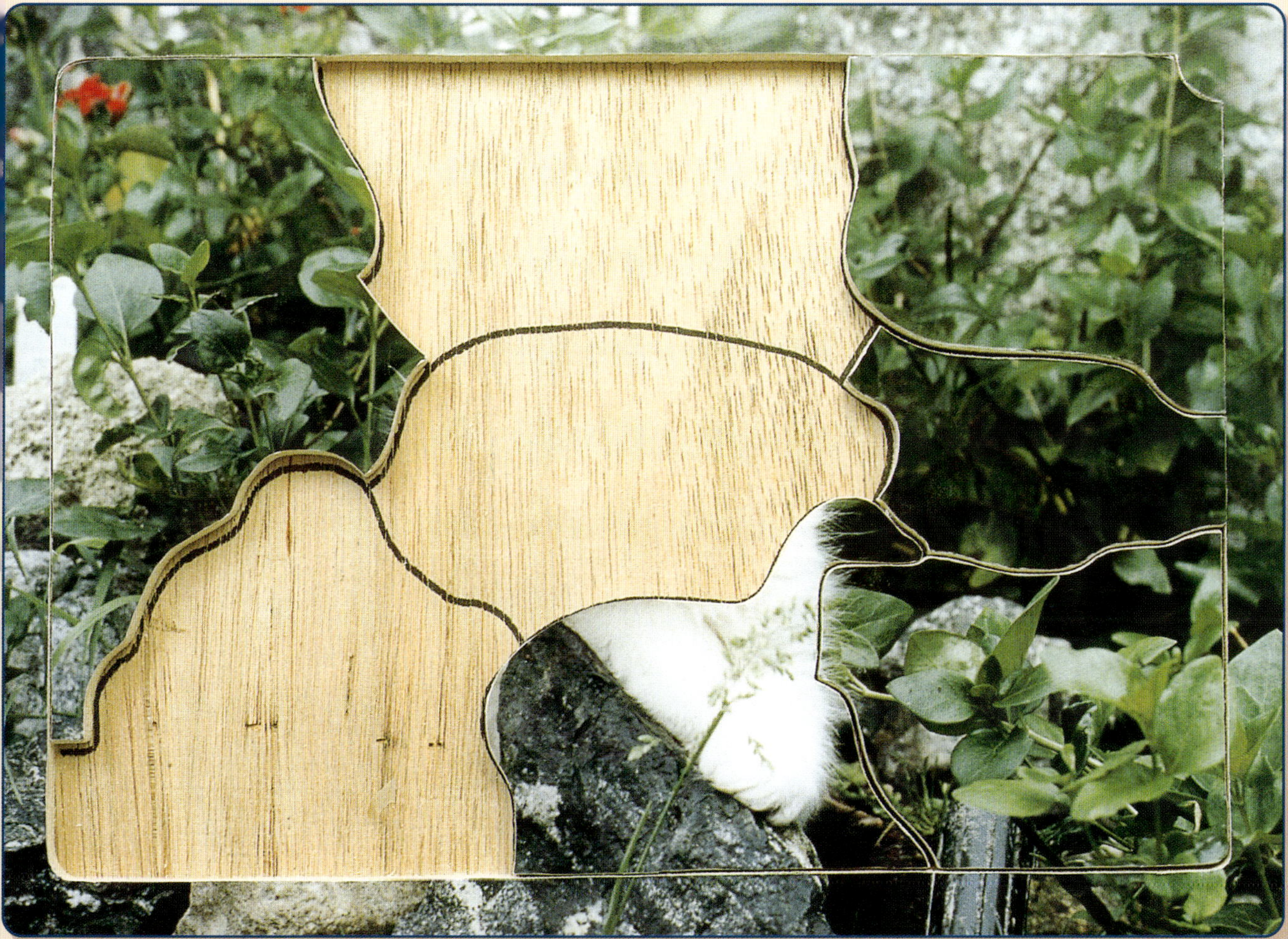

It goes here.

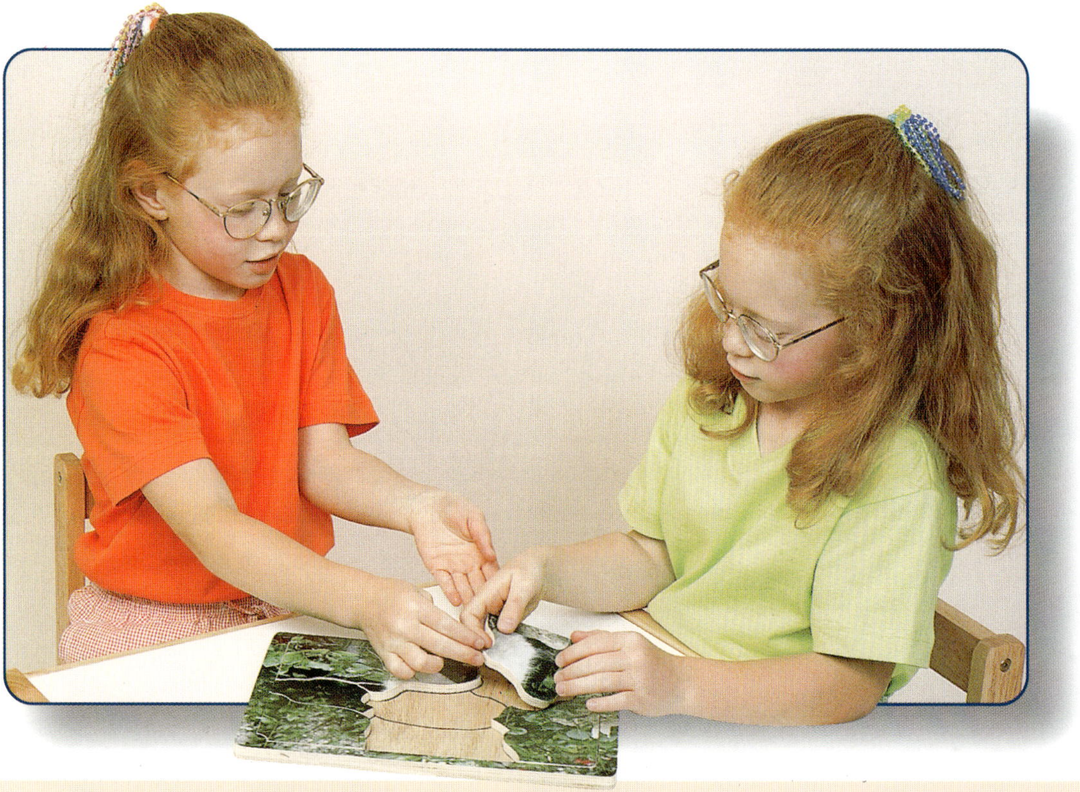

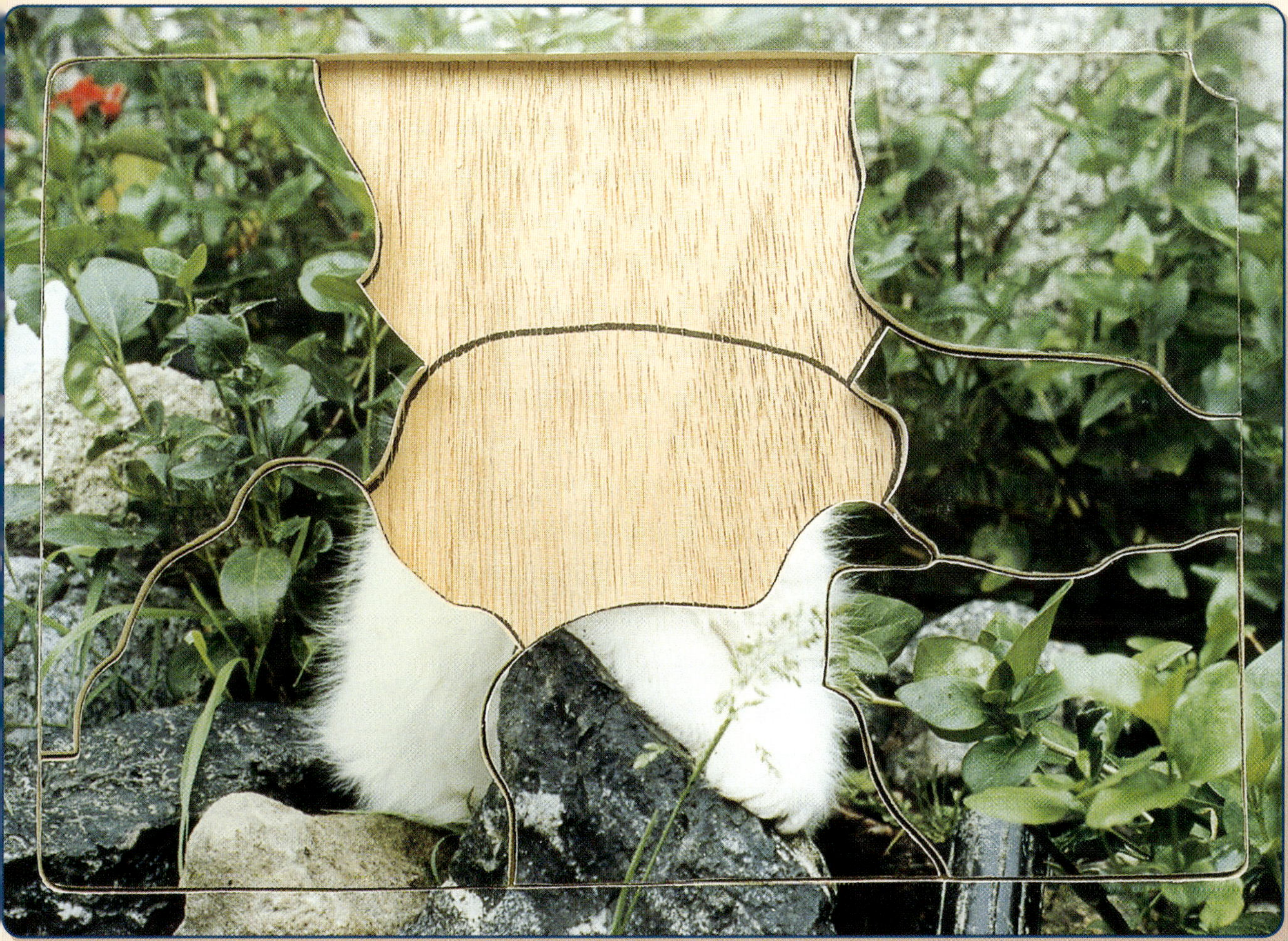

Where does this go?

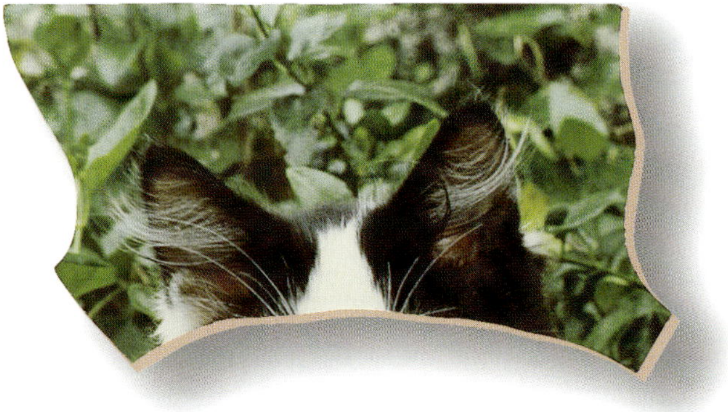

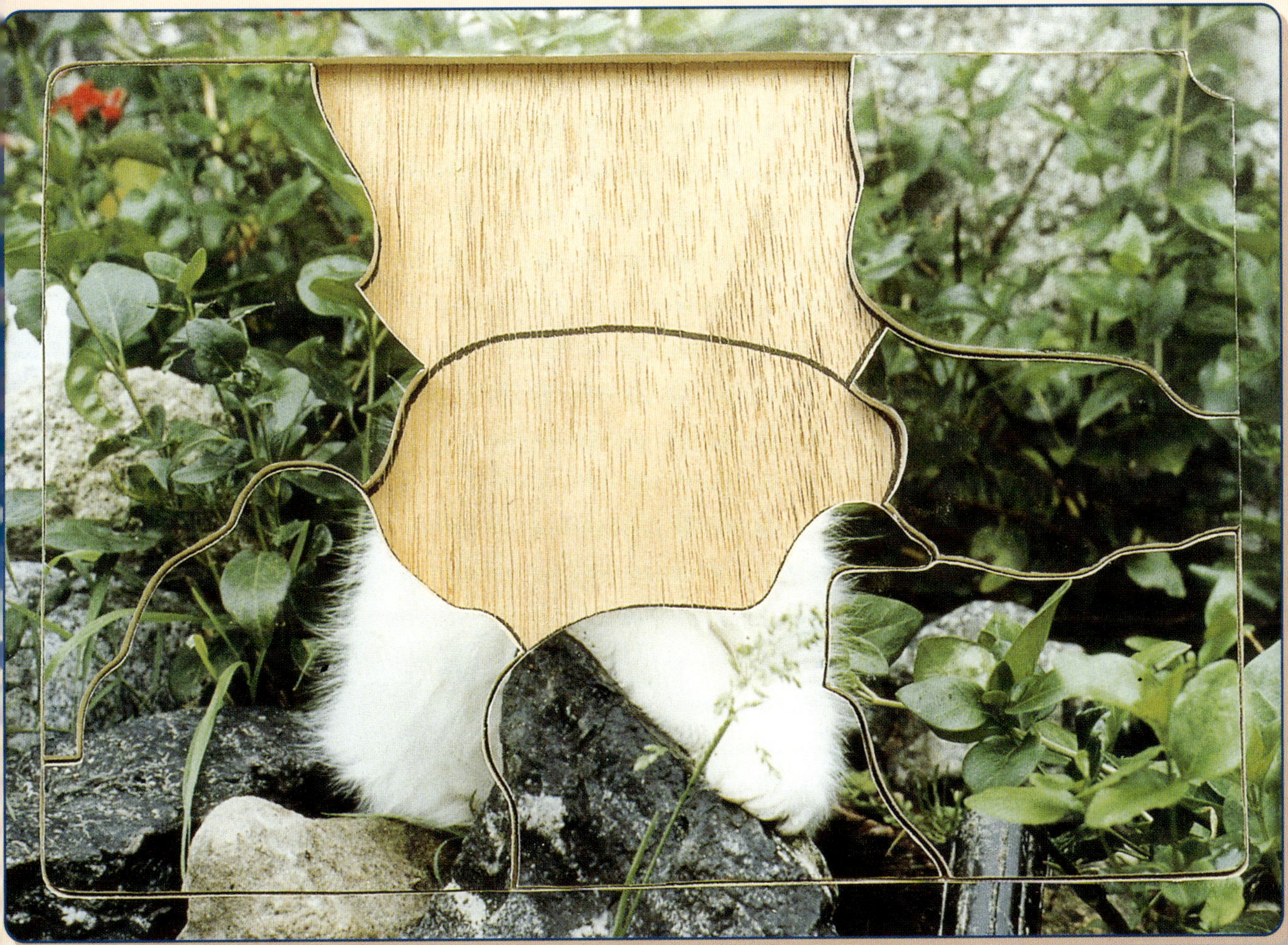

It goes here.

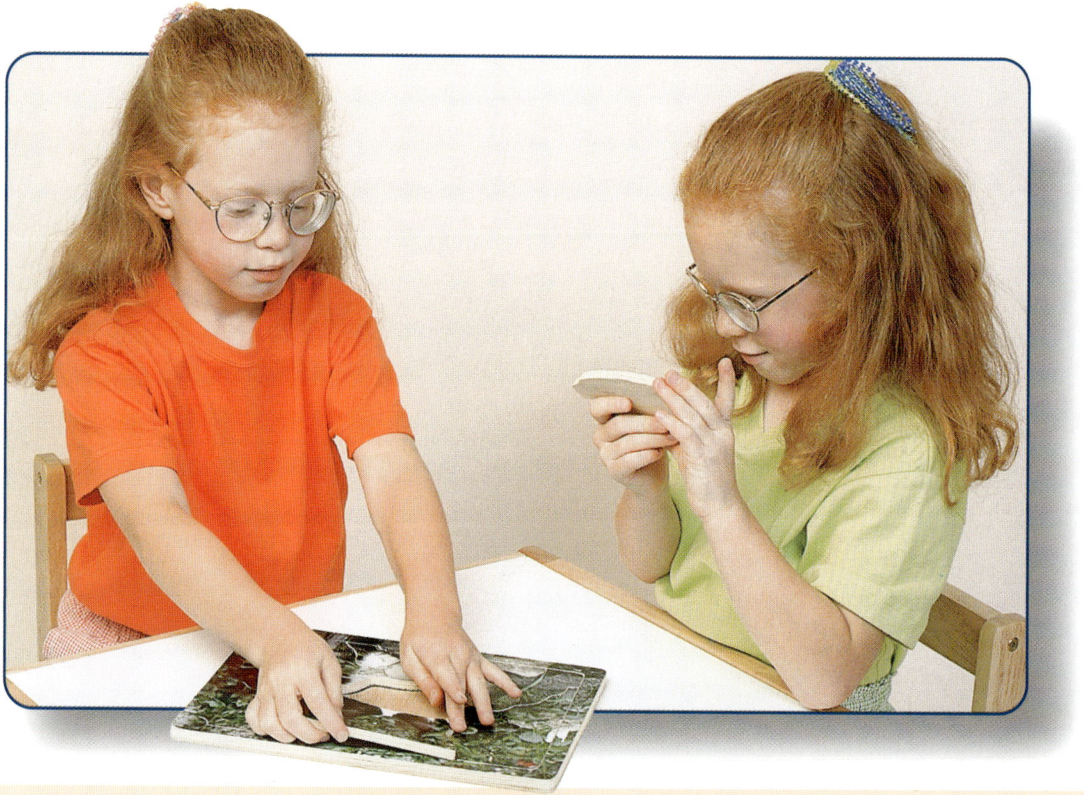

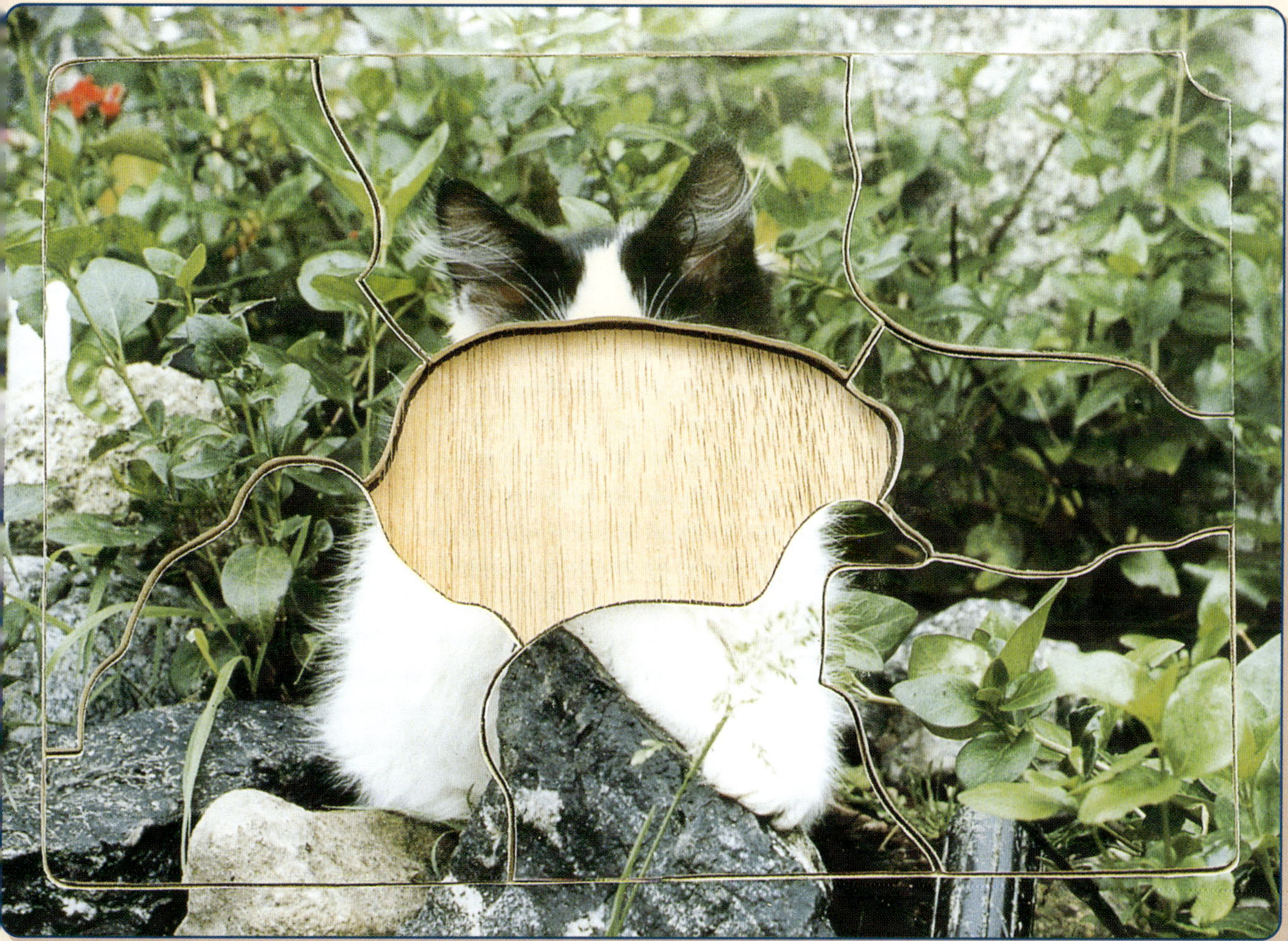

Where does this go?

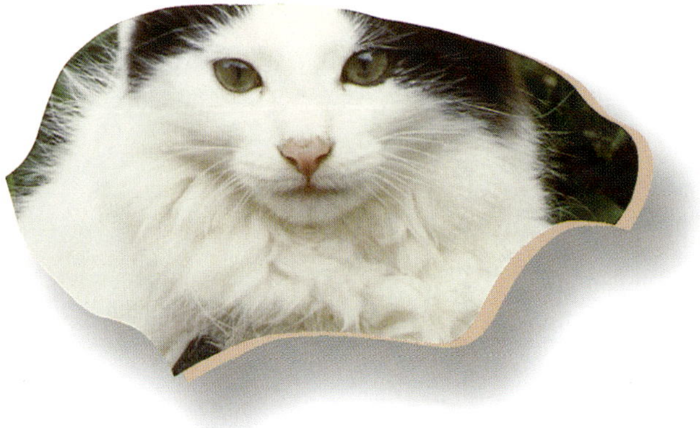

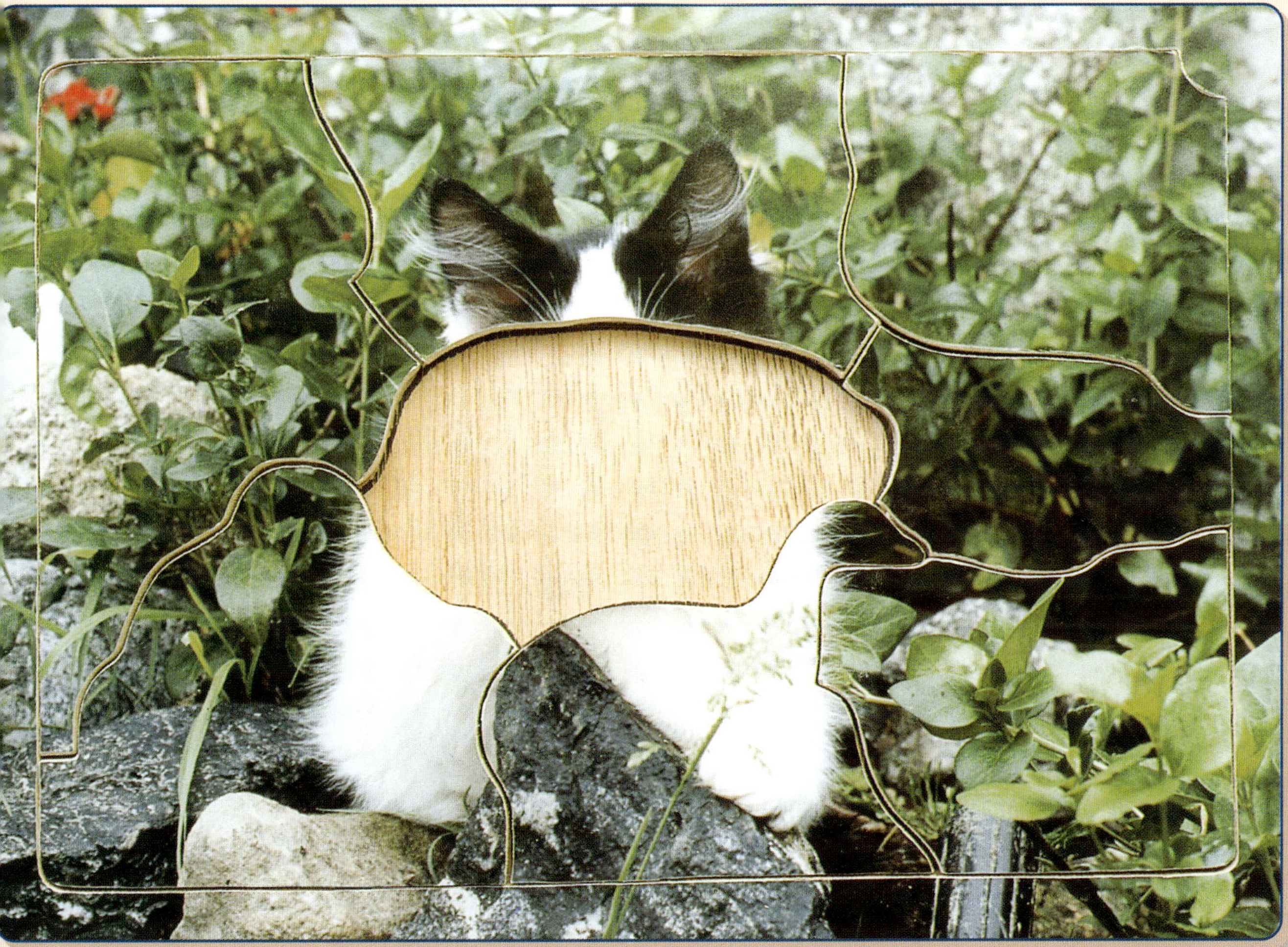

It goes here!

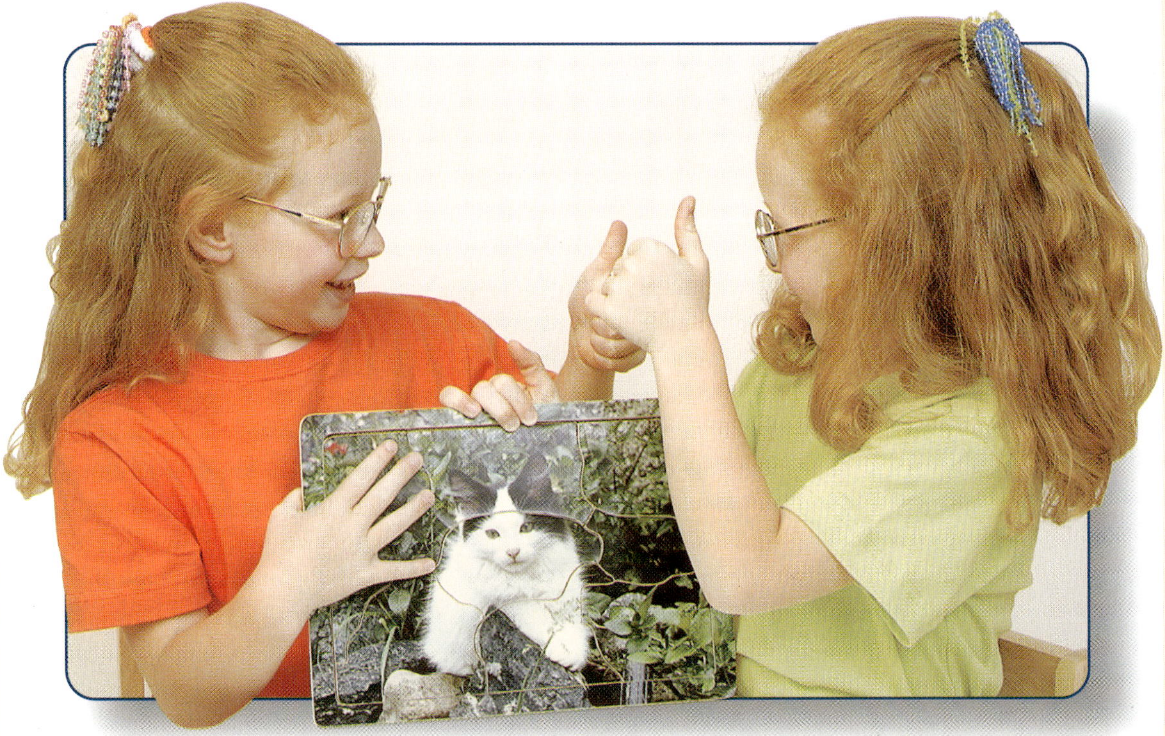